Holy Winter
20/21

ALSO BY MARIA STEPANOVA

In Memory of Memory

Maria Stepanova

HOLY WINTER
20/21

translated by Sasha Dugdale

A NEW DIRECTIONS
PAPERBOOK ORIGINAL

Manufactured in the United States of America
First published as a New Directions Paperbook (NDP1598) in 2024
Design by Erik Rieselbach

Library of Congress Cataloging-in-Publication Data
Names: Stepanova, Maria, author. | Dugdale, Sasha, translator.
Title: Holy winter 20/21 / Maria Stepanova ; translated by Sasha Dugdale.
Other titles: Sviashchennaia zima 20/21. English
Description: New York : New Directions Publishing, 2024.
Identifiers: LCCN 2024004519 | ISBN 9780811235143 (paperback) |
ISBN 97808115150 (ebook)
Subjects: LCGFT: Poetry.
Classification: LCC PG3488.T4755 S8513 2024 |
DDC 891.71/5—dc23/eng/20240202
LC record available at https://lccn.loc.gov/2024004519

2 4 6 8 10 9 7 5 3 1

New Directions Books are published for James Laughlin
by New Directions Publishing Corporation
80 Eighth Avenue, New York 10011

I

I set off on a journey to Russia in the
midst of winter. The country
was covered with snow.

*The Adventures
of Baron Munchausen*

What a winter towering in the yards
Like an oak
Like a stump
Like a shrine

Airborne particles of frost-ash
Tiny cavalry officers
Circling the guilty head
Diving on its very dome

Time for hibernation.

As an undone corpse subsides where it is slain;
Inexorable as the gathering pace of a train
Lie then, where you are laid
For the rules are already made.

There was once a hare, and once a vixen
And they lived by the deep blue sea.
First they lived in an ancient dugout
But then they both built homes

The vixen built a house of ice
And I've heard the hare's was of mica
Built from timid hare-tears
And sad cabbage saliva

And so they lived in harmony, hare and fox
On holy days they set off fireworks.

—I had a dream: In my dream a table, and on it
Lay the most wondrous youth
And he was arrayed in
Palest attire, sable shroud.
—Little Mother, most gracious Majesty!
—My marble-hewn hero.
My own darling, quite beyond compare
How I love you. Wait and see.

Then everything went to sleep:
The wind in the chimney, the fire in the hearth,
And an ache in a head, and the water in the tap.

Then everything stopped still:
The hairdresser at the end of a shift in her overalls
Her legs stretched out, eyes half-shut
And the homeless man in the stationary streetcar
And traffic lights, switched to amber

And in the winter air the police batons
And the yellow sky supported by pillars of smoke
And people in furs in hats in police vans
And people apprehended at their registered address
Their almost transparent houseplants
Their speechless domestic animals
Their warm clothes, their cold drinks
We, wrapped in snow for safe-keeping
Like pictures overlaid with glassine,
Suddenly came to a stop.

I remember when I was packing to leave, for life
That first time I felt my spirit dumb within me
As if it knew what it would now have to learn
And my wife wept, and my two friends, the bravest ones,
But my daughter was away, she'd come home to find me gone.
Dawn broke—and half the night spent burning manuscripts
    and documents.
I took no clothes, I chose no slaves to take with me.
When I think back I find myself already on the ship
The sea all around me, the sea on the decks,
The helmsman prays, the water roars, sailors swear,
My nostrils fill with waves but I write on
Let's see what tires first, the storm, or my appeal.

How did we come to be in this wardrobe?
(How did I come to be in this coffin?)

We aren't alone in the wardrobe:
Ancient shaggy pelts,
A frozen fleece, hung with icicles
Fur coats with deep dark shores
You are lost in them (we are lost) as in a forest
The dreadful smell of chill, nightfall
The snow marked by the pox.

In a distant and strange realm
There rocks a crystal tomb,
Snow falls, starlit space
The coffin swaying side to side
Above the earth in a wasted place
On a bed of ice sleeps your bride.

Marie Stahlbaum dreams
That she is in a deep well—
The sleeve of her father's fur coat
The musk of mothballs, closeness, darkness
The silken lining whispering,
Walls lined with jars and jars
Filled with summer fruit preserve
Whitest light at the end of the tunnel
The staircase gets steeper and steeper
The steps fewer and fewer.

Tatiana Larina dreams
That she is running out to meet you
But the earth has long grown cold
The colonnaded house knee-deep
In heaped snow

The path gone, the road under drifts
That reach to the steeple's cross.
No headstones anymore, the churchyard
Full, and the rosy tint of the snow,
Pale as drugget opened over the plain.

No, we can't take the sleigh and ride out
To the pine woods for tea with Mr. Bear.

Ovid in Tomis dreams
Of white geese over Rome.

Auntie Toma dreams
Of how the model life begins.

If you in the megapolis remember me still, the exiled one,
Know this: I died as my sentence was spoken.
I live like the dead, I wear my body thin
Pliant it shrinks to my bones.
I'm an outsider here, a barbarian, deaf to the language
An idler, my hair white at my temples
I mouth the Getic tongue with dead lips
With dead legs I stamp the stiffened water.
What can I tell you, my wife, to lessen your pain? How horses
Gallop over the smooth river, arrows are let loose;
How fish cling fast-bound in the ice, their mouths agape
And there is no one to free them. Nor to understand me.

The wine freezes and stays in its shape even without the jug
I break a small fragment and suck on it like a nipple.
There are no apples. You wouldn't recognize me now.
The locals are wrapped up in pelts with only their faces
    uncovered
Though thickly bearded. They look askance at my toga.
Even the stars here are not mine.

Liber, little book, written in time's hidden pocket,
In lands where such as we are faint wraiths,
Go now to the limelight of the City
Where every word wears a handsome purple fringe
Go unshaven, your coat worn and faded
Your lamed feet, your cheek stained by tears.
Go to that place where misfortune is not known
Where there is no square I have not kissed in my mind's eye.
You are to say only that I live, no more.
Let them ask questions if they wish—
Only a few will, all the while glancing about them.
Bear in mind that others will want to injure you
But it hardly matters: to reach the hand of a reader,
I would roll up into a scroll, carry myself to the post office.

—Little Mother, most gracious Majesty!
—Dearest invaluable friend
My own sweet darling
Cherished soul!
Giaour, Muscovite, Yaik Cossack,
Pugachev, Turkey cock, Peacock
Tomcat-from-over-the-seas, Golden pheasant
Tiger, Lion in a reed bed
You are beyond compare. I spit on the rest.

A winter morning. Dawn
Light flickers over the rafters.
She rises
Reluctant
From her bed
Wraps a dressing gown around her.
Wipes her pocket mirror with a sleeve.
At this hour, no one to see. No
Need for face-paint so early.

Want to know how to build a house out of snow?
An igloo
A glass dome
An ice palace without walls or roofs?

The boy hid.
Dug out a burrow in the light snow
Climbed in and dragged his sledge in after him
Began heaping up the entrance with handfuls of snow, higher
    and higher.
Blue twilight spilled into his lair.
Can't see you. Can't see you.

The boy dreams
Of a cardboard box filled with dolls' gloves
The parting in her tawny hair, head bent over the tablecloth
Gray eyes glancing reproachfully
Oval portraits of great-grandmother and great-grandfather.

If you squat down and grip your legs behind the knees
And then, with a sudden leap, stretch yourself tall, and lie flat in
    the air
You can swim almost without paddling your hands
Over the leather sofa, the yellow carved sideboard
Into the summer quarters of the house.

But do you need to when you have a sledge?

Darkness fell.
Snowflakes, flying strictly sideways, never downwards
Angled themselves at the cathedral bell tower
And the rider in the handsome sleigh, in snow-white furs
Nodded and nodded at the little boy
Like a china dog.
The little boy had long since opened his hands and let go
But his little sledge
Slid forward of its own accord, following the mysterious rider.
Behind them whirled tiny feathered white hens,
Brilliant lakes of snow lit their way
Wolves howled, the snow clouds bounded above.

So cold, so very cold and deserted!
One day she would kiss him.

Back on the ship, in December, at the very beginning
When it hurt just as much, but everything was still new,
I noticed that the winter was reckoning with me
Testing on its tooth the warmth that remained to me.
The winds were icy, I made conversation with them—
After all I had nobody else—and then the cold suddenly spoke:
"Still writing the poems, old fool? Well keep writing, if you must."
And I, thinking I could strike a bargain: "What if I put an end to it,
Would you leave me be then? No more literature, no more poetry
Nothing good ever came of it, here I am rocking on the black
   waters
For the sake of poems. Would you cease blowing in through my
   lips, snatching at my bones?"
I thought I'd deceived winter, but she'd sucked me in;
No sooner had we made land she was leafing through my ribs,
   through pages in my notebook
As in a police raid, making up her charge sheet.
Now I see I am exiled—not to distant lands
But thrust deep into a season, like a sleeve
On one of the stinking fur coats they wear round here.
And everyone I meet is an exile
Thrown into the damp sackcloth of winter.

We were separated by a storm in the latitude of 73, insomuch that only the ship which I was in, with a Dutch and French vessel, got safe into a creek of Nova Zembla. We landed, in order to refit our vessels, and store ourselves with provisions. The crew of each vessel made themselves a cabin of turf and wood. We soon observed, that in talking to one another we lost several of our words, and could not

hear one another at above two yards' distance, and that too when we
sat very near the fire. After much perplexity, I found that our words
froze in the air before they could reach the ears of the persons to whom
they were spoken. I was soon confirmed in this conjecture, when, upon
the increase of the cold, the whole company grew dumb, or rather
deaf. For every man was sensible, as we afterwards found, that he
spoke as well as ever, but the sounds no sooner took air than they were
condensed and lost. It was now a miserable spectacle to see us nodding
and gaping at one another, every man talking, and no man heard.

I remember everything just as it was
And even that today is poetry day in the City.
I've lost the art myself: poems are the toys of the fortunate
Who like to play at misfortune.
But still, thinking of you all rushing about
From one poetry reading to the next
The taste of wine in your mouths, your wreaths still green—
Not one of you would stem the tide of confessional lyric
Slam your glass down on the table to ask "How's our mate Naso
    getting on?"
Or even "Here's to all those at sea!"

Oh how I'd like to spit a few frozen iambs
Blunt as the points of arrows in these parts—
The only souvenirs manufactured around here.

Will it be here I lie, dry earth, in you?
Where only the medicinal clumps of wormwood straggle on.
No wayside monument on the Appian, no altar
No roaring funeral fire, no weeping mourner
Even the auspicious birds can't be summoned from so far.
A pauper's funeral: quick, tidy, cost effective.
The plow hasn't the means for the stony earth
The stony water is painted to look like marble.
The Greek spoken here is as cracked as a biscuit in your pocket
No one speaks Latin, and that's probably for the best,
They'll say in their own tongue:
"The old man had had enough"—now let him be.

They say
That a snowstorm over the forum
Laid its white linen on the benches.

They say
That skyscrapers in far distant lands
Were pictures curtained in snow.

That between the columns of the Parthenon
Lodged little drifts like fur hats.

Never before had such a thing happened—and then it did.

Night. Winter.
I was deep in a book,
Forgot it was time for bed.
My wife came and took the lamp:
"Do you know how late it is?"

Could be three years, or even thirty three
Could be ten, like the Greeks at the walls of Troy
It's much the same—time stands still
Like a man locked up, every new day like the last,
Nights cut from the same cloth, shoddy dreams:
Rain falling like arrows, snow like string, a slave's lot.
I look up—my eyelashes are frozen, salt on my fingertips,
Only this way do I realize I have been crying.
My dreams are not of Cupid with his little frozen wings
Nor of the spring thaw and the first letter brought by boat.

If I were in my rightful mind I would think perhaps of Rome
Of the rain-dampened laurel, and the light from the house
Or I'd remember shop signs
And my nose would prickle with tears and the heat of garum.
Or I might think of embracing you
My hand feeling its way over your shoulder blades
And coming to a fearful stop, no longer recognizing your skin.
Or even: how the storm rattles at the gates locked fast against
    foes.

But instead my thoughts return shamefully to my works
And how they have broken my life apart,
And I wonder if anyone still reads you, my poor little books.
I want you out of my mind, I want you limping away,
Little uneven heaps, fire-scorched remnants,
To the library of classic works,
I've been holding your tongue for far too long.

Under Ursa Major in winter, from under its star-pocked coat,
I grieve over the cosmic shift.
Can it be true that one of the earthbound gods is gone
And all the hierarchies of power upended?
To whom now should I lift up my voice
In prayers for a pardon?
Neither you nor I quite know
Why I write, although people say poets are mad.
Between my writing and your seeing
Is a season, always the same one: cold
And eternal snowfall and the breadth of Thrace
And many many watery leagues.
In icy winter the fish live under a crust
And so do I. I close my mouth in the darkness
And hold my own tongue, I have two more now to choose from:
Getic and Sarmatian, both newly acquired.
In neither do I wish to dip a toe.

—I harbor in me not a single untender thread.
Tenderness will fill any space that is left to it.
The nature of my own tenderness is that of a busybody
Always fussing about, whenever she is not pushed away
And when she is pushed away
Then she spins round like a demon
Looking for a place
Where she can take up her post.
Yaur, Muscovite, Cossack, wolf, bird.
—My Little Mother, most gracious Majesty!

A little like this: instead of coming out of the closet
They crowd inside it, and find themselves somewhere else.
Or they only went briefly into this wardrobe
But heard the key turn behind them—
And now they're in another place,
The morning snow under the tips of their slippers.

Or perhaps they didn't even know it was a wardrobe, until
The door slammed shut, the light slowly grew
And it was suddenly clear—we're in another place,
Naphthalene sprinkling down from above.
Emptiness, like war, like revolution
On the city's squares and in the streets
Like an epidemic, or the world cup final—
And the morning snow falling from above.

Now everything can be seen, how it all happens at once:
A light glowing in every apartment, and at the same time
Each man in his closet sits at his table, waters his houseplant
Stands, sits, lies, leaves the light burning
Shines blinding bright like a lamp in the small hours
Like girls in the windows of red light districts
With no one to see them, the streets are empty,
And the naphthalene falls softly.

Lonely, bloated, drooping like paunches,
These balloons hanging in the air:
Aerial wardrobes on invisible strings
Filled with un-laughing gas.
In dark water, made of ice and water
Rose the many stories of phosphorescent fish.
In the winter sky, made of snow and sky,
Gleamed the windows of many-storied buildings
Empty shops, piled high with goods
Restaurants with the chairs leaned against the tables
Offices with last year's calendar
Fixed on the page with March's girl
And from above fell the morning light.

Sometimes fauns came out onto the ice
Downy dark wool
On thin little hooves
Fearing
To leave too many
Cloven prints on the white.

On the top of Etna
Words congeal in the mouth,
Speech crunched in the cheek
Like teeth knocked out in a fight—

So Messer Leonardo notes
In his prized moleskine.

Most ingenious Petronius
Says: in the middle of the world
There's a pole, like a maypole
With a dovecot at its top
And in that dovecot
Words flutter, peck and foul,
And thoughts and images from
Past and future centuries
Squabble, slovenly, copulate
Produce chicks.

And when husks and foulness spill over
They fall straight into the squawking mouths
Of witnesses, standing around the pole:

Go home! Go digest
The present tense!

We can't hear the birds
But we know they are there.

This winter is like being in that thick forest with the golden bough
Where the golden priest ministers to the golden oak
(For "golden," read "white")—
Or like being in the labyrinth with Pasiphae's boy
Nowhere to go until the next shift arrives
And knocks the horned head clean from its human forequarters.
I won't object, I won't resist, not even for the sake of form,
Nor wave a sword, although the weapon here
Is just an item of homeware, without it you can't make your way
Out for a piss, even I have a pocketful.
I feel already the weight of this head, the dilating nostrils
Where once I spoke, now just usss, yuuu, iiice.
Soon another ghost of a man will appear in my wake
And learn in time to make the local sounds
And clear the snow from the porch
And how trousers made of pelts are shaming, but warm.

The evening fit to burst. The glass empty.
My head empty. Warmth in my chest
If time has a pocket
Then place me in it, gently.
Dimmed light, a sugar cone
Night-time conversation, a shadowy man.
The check came, but we settled scores
Wanting better tempora, better mores.

We have a gift. Some call us
The best poets of our age.
Our apartments alas are humbler than our fame
And even our fame amounts to fuck all.
Starving servants, dressed in rags
Regard us with disdain. The two of us
Hardly old—and look at our wrinkles!
Still, who cares less about us
Or our woes? We are
Our own readers, we know
Our own and each other's worth.
Our texts will be placed in a deep ditch
With the work of the great dead poets—
That's how we console ourselves, anyway.
At least we won't die childless.

When the time comes to cross the waters—
Not here, where the river's mouth clouds the sea
So even winter's jade light is drowned—
But that crossing we all make, together with everything we know
Even then we'll be divided into lines for boarding
According to our mother tongues:
The language we swear in in our dreams.
So my shade will stand separate from the rest
Under the sign marked "Citizens of R.E."
At passport control,
And the people here will form a different line
Quite apart from me, not even looking my way.
Well, of course, they don't speak our tongue,
When I speak they suppress laughter
And my lingua spills over like a sauce
No one wants to taste.
Yes, their hair hangs long, their furs are mangy
Their arrows, their bristling cheeks, their half-hidden eyes
And nothing to make small talk about at the shop
Because the weather is always the same
And it's clear I'd be useless in their home guard.
But even when we are naked and hairless shades—
All these Getae and a single Roman
Waiting for the steamship—still no one will stand
Close enough for their warmth to heat my left flank.

Cold, oh the Cold!
The casement windows must be open somewhere.
Giaour, Muscovite, Cossack.
Cossack, Muscovite, son of a bitch.

II

I beheld that the wolf had ate his way into
the horse's body. The poor animal ran
the faster for its pain and terror.

*The Adventures
of Baron Munchausen*

A stirring, ceaseless
Tickling
And scratching
Water on snow
Steam on water
Self on self

And dark, as the inside of a bucket

And like steamed-up glasses
Like in the brightest bath of snow
You are made double
You evaporate as you move

And everything, crackling
As if a fingernail was tapping on

Tell me, sovereign of my heart, how things are and whether I am in
your favor?

The Godhead is angry with me, I made an error
An error, I can't say what. What it was I can't say
An error—and where now, here now, here

Better not to attract the anger of one
Whose power is equal with that of the gods
And if you do attract his anger better hope
That his mercy is also equal with that of the gods—
But which gods? Which of the gods was noted for mercy?
I made an error, a mistake, and by mistake I erred
But what was my error, I don't know
Can only guess that maybe it was
The same error that another committed, and another, too—
I won't name them here, because that would be
Unforgivable, an unforgivable mistake

Even in my unearned and errant
New world. I loved:
The City. The spring, the sudden crowds promenading;
The divan in the summer house, when the curtains breathed;
Myself, when I was with you. It was an error,
I was amiss—a mistake—mistook me, yet did I err?
Around me men wearing cold weapons
And nowhere, not for any money, can I find a proofreader.

And what to do when you can do nothing?
We sing and we sweat, both bodily functions.
Convicts sing, long distance truckers, loaders
A seamstress at her machine sings under her breath
As I do: I sing to myself. I read myself to myself,
Sometimes I think: you nailed it, you bastard! or I'm a genius!
I'm old but I keep going, gray, but I'm still at it
As if it wasn't my poems that got me holed up in the Far North
As if those who never answered my letters
Took an interest in those who sang, wanting them kept alive,
As if literature was indeed the most vital of all the arts
And Caesar himself, before retiring to his chambers
Would ask his secretary: any news from Naso?
What's he scribbling in that Voronezh of his?

—Love shut away in the heart with ten sturdy locks
How horribly constrained she is in there
Confined in great misery
Watch out, for one day she will leap free.

What the god—what the hero—what the fuck
I could shovel my Heroides into Sarmatian,
Manure the thin steppe-soil with it
The ferment of cultural expansion:
After all, where I am, there too is Rome—snow, the purest
    marble
And isn't my own homeland the Greek tragedies?
I could do a job on the Getic myths of origin
(A few tall tales about a cosmic eel)
Parcel them up nicely in a couplet
Lay them out for your perusal as colonial wares
Alongside honey from Hymettus or Germanic boar pate.
I could open a village school,
Depict the histories of historic women
Thrown casually aside by gods or heroes:
Dido on the beach, Ariadne on the beach,
And you—who sank down on the threshold
As they led me away—and lay there.

(D)

You, whoever you were: a refugee, forgot your name
Or even where you came from, carried on your family's back
Little piss-pants, your father always on about how
He was once some big shot in the Veterans' Office
You mixing up words, always on the lookout, ready to draw
If it hadn't been for me and my strip of farmed land
My widow's capital, where would you have been
Would you even have been.

When I lay with you, I lay as if in a small boat,
As if in the winter sea I lay, and slowly
Learned to see, through the wreck of your hull
The slow procession of sea monsters
The hulks of sunken cruise ships
The thrum of the motor as immigration draws alongside
Demanding all hands on deck and no resistance—
And I showed no resistance.

But still we went down. And you emerged onto dry land
Under different constellations, you lost your fins
Grew lungs and left me there in the sand:
Driftwood, driftqueen, drifting boat.
And if I want to give chase—to catch you
I must make myself to fire and air, like the Egyptian
So the smell of me clings in your nostrils, and you wish to dispel it
But can't.

(A)

I wake on the white, the empty white island
Of the bed you have already left
And know then that you have abandoned me
And know, too, that I am an island.
He who said no man is an island
Never lay isolated in a lonely bed
Where white sheets heralded the winter as it fell
Between lines of text; where, between you and me,
Only whiteness, the unseen intervals between metro trains

The wide avenues unpeopled, the squares where we are not,
And no connective tissue, no silken threads
To catch hold of and cling to,
No balls of words coiled neatly for another to catch:
A man, imprisoned in his own flesh
And another, escaping his captivity
Not wishing to be part of the archipelago
Nor the federal republic clinched in embrace
Nor the zone where territories meet
For all these lay bare the scar for all to see:
His island nature. I see cliffs on the coast.

The God of Love pierced me with his stinger
The God of Sleep couldn't keep me in my cradle
But the God of Alcohol comes to my aid
Caresses me from within, his sprouting thyrsus anesthetizes.

(O)

It would be good to know what form you'll take
In that place where all the forms have been worn to death
And bodies surrendered for recasting—no one recognizes
    anyone
Even you are no longer known by the claws on your lion pelt.
When we were together we were whatever we wanted to be.
You only had to say,
                        and that's how it was: our blithe fluidity
Entering all the body's openings like the sea.
I was a general and a fluttering bird all at once

A general and an army; generalissima and samovar;
And you were a lion with its claws; a girl at her spinning wheel
Hoplite at the Hauptwache; wet diaper, dung beetle,
Movable feast. You wore my skirt, I wore your fatigues
I stopped shaving my legs, you pissed sitting down
So we travestied all the workings of power,
Screw gender, its two halves hollowed,
And we, simultaneous and plural, took turns at
Mommy and Daddy, maple and quickbeam, general and bird.
But never just you and me:
An elderly officer in a provincial backwater
And a little local woman, blessed with inventiveness—
Such tactics eased our parting,
And I am confident I won't recognize you there.

—How cold you are, so cold!
My dearest spinning-top
Your indisposition puts my soul out of sorts.

Writers of literature referring
To strange circumstances
And desiring to emphasize their strangeness, say:
This has never happened before. It will never happen again.
Often they reach for the same image
It is as if (they write) in an ordinary room
Snow began to fall
Slowly covering both divan and writing desk.

Writers of books and film scripts
Make the snow fall—not where you'd expect it
But where it has no place falling
In the grand halls of museums, on coastal palm trees
Between the columns of the Parthenon
On squares in Rome
In the lounges of empty airports.

Now snow is everywhere, its absence unthinkable
Casting its light on the unnatural union
The fearful coitus of the impossible
And our lives, as they have come to be.
And how strangeness once again claims its own.

Emptiness does much the same
Where her foot has not hitherto trod
On squares in Rome, in departure lounges,
Folding seats in cinemas
In hospitals where relatives are forbidden
Locked cemeteries, in public toilets.
Emptiness now stretches herself out
And poses for photographs.

And there is another, a third presence,
For his sake everything is covered over with white

But the children have all been sent to the nursery.
His boots squeak. Look closer—
We see nothing.

We continued here three weeks in this dismal plight. At length, upon a turn of wind, the air about us began to thaw. Our cabin was immediately filled with a dry clattering sound, which I afterwards found to be the crackling of consonants that broke above our heads, and were often mixed with a gentle hissing, which I imputed to the letter S, that occurs so frequently in the English tongue. I soon after felt a breeze of whispers rushing by my ear; for those, being of a soft and gentle substance, immediately liquefied in the warm wind that blew across our cabin. These were soon followed by syllables and short words, and at length by entire sentences, that melted sooner or later, as they were more or less congealed; so that we now heard everything that had been spoken during the whole three weeks that we had been silent, if I may use that expression. It was now very early in the morning, and yet, to my surprise, I heard somebody say, "Sir John, it is midnight, and time for the ship's crew to go to bed." This I knew to be the pilot's voice, and upon recollecting myself I concluded that he had spoken these words to me some days before, though I could not hear them before the present thaw.

(P)

What do I have: a home, a son, these embroidery hoops, a dog
A dark cool hall with a view to the sea
Marble streaked with the midday sun
Corned beef kept in crates in the cellar
For every fourth year, when the harvest fails.
If you find him, little letter, ask him this:
Did I even once beg him to stay?

I'm doing fine. Much like my friends
One husband went to town to find work and
Vanished, another enlisted as a mercenary and he too:
Gone. My life is like theirs
I hum as I do the housework
I dance as I lay the table for dinner, for
Personal contentment consists in having few mouths to feed.

How the clumsy cold winds rummage in the waves,
And sometimes out of the waves rises an unbidden dream
A one-eyed eater, hunter of our flesh,
A stone that speaks, an isle of serpents,

A witch who turns men into pigs
And lets them perish in the waters.

Did I even once ask you to come back?
I never asked them to come, those men
Who pay me coins for their double, no ice,
Nor for their talk of my eternal feminine.
I hardly have time to wash my feet
In the dusk of evening, to sit briefly alone
On the darkening terrace.

But every morning, before I wipe over
The cafe tables and draw out the awning
I weave the weather forecast:
The blinding blue of the Ocean
Boreas with armfuls of snow, dimpled Zephyrus
Scylla's jaws, the princess with her ball.
The Golden Fleece, which has nothing to do with anything.
Sleepy young conscripts on watch duty
Not shot, but throttled to death
The freight of trophies in foreign ports.
Women's feet, their slim ankles.

I stitch and unwind the road back home.
Every morning my forecast changes.

—Little Mother, Most gracious Majesty,
Little Mother, I am so unwell.
My own little mother
I don't know what will become of me.

(A different A)

Lights out. The girls disperse to their tents
Clean their weapons, check their ammo:
All in order. You ask how I am
I'm battle ready.
No point in crying over spilt milk
Or a pierced shield, or a life suspended
Like a plush monkey on a string
Jigging up and down, back and forth.
Your place now is a dark and empty place, your sleeping bag
Left folded under a layer of dust, and it's as if you never were.
You say that warriors also cry—
Like the man in Asia Minor crying over his boy
Who went out on reconnaissance without him
And came back with a severed head.

You ask how I am. I have forgotten you.
I don't ask how you are—man-boy, man-son,
New country, new passport, new war
Old hands in armed conflict zones
A sniper shooting at her former friends.
I thought you just a small and graceless girl.
Now we both have a different fate.
Quicker than stripping and reassembling a machine gun
The memory of me gathers and scatters
In your disfigured breastless breast.
Tomorrow morning we take up our positions
And you will earn your posthumous medal
And I will enter into deathless afterlife.

At about half a mile's distance from our cabin, we heard the groanings of a bear, which at first startled us; but upon inquiry we were informed by some of our company, that he was dead, and now lay in salt, having been killed upon that very spot about a fortnight before, in the time of the frost. Not far from the same place we were likewise entertained with some posthumous snarls and barkings of a fox.

(I)

The girls all say of me: Poor I
O, what's biting you, darling
My boi calls me his babe, his girl
His ex calls me "it" or "that cow"
But I see in myself almost nothing
Of what they ascribe to me.
The last few months I've been beside myself
Wandering from bar to bar, from high to low,
I scrounge cigarettes from shopkeepers
Stand watch over frozen rubbish dumps
As if I were collecting empty bottles, or looking for bentwood
    chairs.
I blunder on: wooden benches in railway carriages,
Little halts in the suburbs with the trampled snow blackened,
Then abysses, blizzard-bent boughs, a well crowned with a
    cardboard icon.
A boarded-up club, a beat-up cafe, a cattle trough.
The blood itches under my pelt, desperate to get out.
Even here there's no room for me: low sky, few fields
I want to run, I don't even know where to—
I throw back my head and sway my haunches
To rid myself of the tickling gadfly of my bloodstream
My strong legs beat the long miles
Ceaselessly, unwearyingly, obliviously
And free-willed, I bellow the song about willow
No words, no tunes, just lowing, io-ing.

Blow winds. A crowd of unknown ghosts.
I sing heartbroken, alone and old, I sing
To myself. The rags of fog hang
In the twilight. A flurry of snow
The wind whistles. My glass of wine
Is gone, the bottle empty.
The fire dwindles in the hearth.
Whoever speaks, speaks in a whisper.
I think about how these letters mean nothing.

At night special ops
Were sometimes seen
Crossing the transparent border
Dispersing into our darkness

How will we know them, friend?
They look just like us

We too cross the border
Onto the other bank
Of the boundary river

Where a campfire burns a light through the fog
Where an open wound bleeds out bull's blood
To warm our lips,
Speech, untying the mouth
Like a sack of chicken bones:
We picked them clean
We left them bare.

They say that in heaven
There are no husbands, no wives
Everyone is naked as the ascending angels
If that's so then we are in heaven
We're in heaven
In barrack 16
Lying on the furthest bunk
We have no memory of husbands, nor wives

You and me just come across the border
But we've forgotten it now

The two of us defending our bunk
Sharing our rations

Stuffing our thin pillow
Our shared pillow
With white down.

(with chicken feathers, you say?
well, okay then.)

There's a high cliff on the far bank
So we can't see what's over there
I've been over, but can't remember

You and me drink from the same mess tin
At night we lick each other's souls
Every morning we assemble outside

We haven't given in, grassed anyone up
But the desire remains: to slink on our bellies
After the warm scent of blood, to the guard
And spill over in sincerity
Locking nothing back

(shame I don't remember anything)

I've heard they come from over there
At night, warm, blooming with blood
They come to steal our memories,
They light fires, lead away our women
To beyond the transparent border
And only one ever returned

(but you don't remember why you came back).

My darling my dearest if I start
To gaze beyond that river, kill me quick.

The plot always thickens in winter
All roads lead right to it.
A thirty-five year old Italian man
Lost in a dark wood
Meets a magic helper
As is customary in a fairy tale
But all the same he descends lower and lower
Soaking up all he sees like a sponge
Until he arrives in that place where everything freezes
Even the sponge.

A sharp-witted boy (we don't know how old he is)
Way too smart for his own good
As is customary in puberty
Comes face to face with the fifth season—
A winter, without walls or a roof
Or any limit the mind can conceive of.
She has already kissed him once
And given him vast promises,
A number of letters formed
Of ice, aqueous, glimmering,
A handful of congealed voices,
A few flattened histories.
If you can construct from them anything to last even a while
As immunity against the flow of time
And the low temperatures
And the pestilence that whirls in the eastern winds,

Then
You will be master of your own fate
All the world will be yours
They shall bear thee up in their hands lest thou dash thy foot
    against a stone.
And I will kiss you again.
I shall give you a pair of Norwegian ice skates.
As long as you make it sound good.

(And he forgot about Gerda and Grandmother and all at home
And sat on the ice examining his treasures)

Lower than the very depths
Lower than the deepest deep
At the lowest point of human misery
The Italian saw a frozen lake
And those who were frozen within, like fish
Scaled with icy tears
Eyes that protruded sharp ice needles
And speech that could neither be gnawed at, nor thawed.
These are the traitors. They are beyond forgiveness.

Who have we betrayed so
That there can be no forgiveness for us?

There are no walls, no roof
Only the Northern Lights
And a few shared histories
Opened anew, like little doors.

Wind. The blue of the mountains invisible
In the twilight, under winter stars
Our little house is covered in snow
I hear the dogs barking
By the village gates
Through snow and wind
Someone is coming home.

Foreign words melt in the cheek
Like sugar cubes.

When the cold abates, the words begin to thaw. But as they thaw they all resound at once, and so cannot be fully understood. Sometimes they speak in different languages, although they are saying more or less the same thing. In this book you can hear these once-frozen and now thawing voices as they multiply in the telling, flushed by translation, crackling in the cold. Some of them belong to Erich Raspe (and his fictional hero, who we mustn't confuse with the historic Baron Munchausen); the fourteenth-century traveler Sir John Mandeville (speaking in the words of Joseph Addison); Hans Christian Andersen; the Russian Empress Catherine II (and her beloved Grigory Potemkin); the exiled Publius Ovidius Naso (and his many translators); and the echo of Kenneth Rexroth, through his translations of the classical Chinese poets, translated into Russian, then back into a different English for this book.

March
21/23

Afterword

I don't remember the seasons of spring, autumn, or summer during the pandemic. It's as if all the time spent in lockdown (two long years) has been condensed into one congealed mass and crusted over with ice: a boundless and featureless winter.

In fact I hardly remember the pandemic at all—not as it really was. There is no way back to that mythological time and space, and like anything that will not come again, it gives rise to a feeling of awful and unnatural nostalgia. The pandemic was a sudden pause, a halted train, and the fact that its carriages were filled with both strangers and people close to me, suffocating and dying, made it unbearable, but also precluded any kind of imagining of the future, any thought of what might come.

It was a time outside time, a little like suddenly finding ourselves on a snow-covered island, from which there was no escape—and in any case nowhere to escape to. The past had been sheared away and was so unattainable that it was hard to recall that it had even existed: surely those cities and airplanes, those recent lives, couldn't be us? The old world, the old life, could only be looked at from afar, at one remove from this imposed purgatory-in-life, with its new rules, one of which was the sensation of finality in what was happening to each of us. Soon we discovered that any actual finality was a very distant prospect.

That time now conjures a sense of nostalgia in me, a combination of tenderness and disgust. I am ashamed of my illusion (although, let's face it, what's the point in being ashamed of one's unfulfilled hopes, even if they were naive) that made me see in the pandemic—which the whole world, perhaps for the first time in human history, lived through collectively, in each other's full sight, on live TV, in the present tense—something of an antidote. What had so frightened me, in the years before the virus, belonged to the past, not the present.

Back then it had seemed as if the twenty-first century, which I was yet to completely inhabit, had begun its inexorable landslide back into the twentieth, from where we had only recently emerged, picking our way painstakingly through the wreckage. Everything began to turn its face toward the past: political slogans; the rhetoric of newspapers; the metaphors my writing colleagues began to employ. Everything was in reverse, addressing the past as if it were the future: as either a desired destination point or a mirror we stared in, unable to tear ourselves away. The bookstores in airports were suddenly full of books about the past, all of them—novels, works of history, memoirs—gazing backwards. The future had become hard to imagine long before the pandemic, and, worse than that, it provoked terror and the desire to look away. Behind us in the last century lay terror, too, but at least that terror was recognizable down to its minute parts. It even seemed as if the knowledge of how it had all come about could help us in some way, could teach us how to behave now in order to evade new misfortune.

I have always considered myself a person born into a post-catastrophe era. Once, it seemed to me as if the worst had already happened and all that was required of me was never to forget: to forget nothing, neither the essential nor the inessential, to be one with those who gathered up the fragments and listened to the voices that weren't heeded in their own time. But at some stage the numbers of those who had fixed their gaze on the twentieth century swelled, and among them appeared some who deemed it both possible and expedient to use it as a model, to try to turn the clock back and to make of violence, fear, and hatred a language in which the state might address its citizens, and the citizens themselves speak to each other. In 2014, when Russia began its war against Ukraine, the twentieth century began its colonization of the present; the past became an active force, capable of changing the world, and changing it for the worst. The catastrophe revealed itself to be ahead of us, and I suddenly saw that all my conscious life had happened in a pre-catastrophe, rather than a post-catastrophe era. Do I need to add that I was not prepared for this?

For a while, during the pandemic, it seemed as if it might give humanity a new start—that it would push out or replace the disaster I anticipated and felt to be already close at hand. At that time I wrote a short essay called "War without an Enemy" in which I mused that if a history without catastrophe was not possible, then perhaps it was better to live through this, catastrophe's new variant, and one which removed all the boundaries between people and gave us a common purpose, a shared sense of resistance—and no ground for sowing mutual hate. Because, after all, how could we hate a virus?

But hatred and the desire to seize, to have and control and to make one's own, was stronger than solidarity, stronger even than fear. The pandemic was over for me on February 24, 2022, the day of Russia's full-scale invasion of Ukraine, and although people around me continued to fall ill, the virus and its dangers suddenly ceased to have any meaning for me. The world passed from one phase of the present into another; this phase still continues, and the future, just as before, cannot be discerned; it seems inconceivable.

During the wintry days of 2021, at my dacha just outside Moscow, I had no inkling of what would come. I was reading Ovid's letters from exile and making them into Russian poems. The letters were written from a place and in times that seemed to the Roman poet to be beyond the pale, unlike anything he knew, and therefore demanded to be described in poems. In his versed letters it was always winter and always war, and the gates to the little settlement on the edge of the known world were locked fast against barbarian attack; the water was firm underfoot and people walked over it, and drove their carts across it. Wine froze in the jug and pieces could be broken off and sucked like a popsicle. The world had become unrecognizable and the language Ovid wrote in was unintelligible to the people he now lived amongst. Eternal winter, unending exile, and constant anxiety over whether anyone in the city he called home remembered him. And all this—together with the sense of sudden and utterly irrevocable change—seemed to me to be a mirror, a distorted mirror, one perhaps made of ice, in which I could see numerous reflections, including my own. That is how, back then, in that brief moment of present tense that lasted as if it would never end, I wrote this book. And now it feels to me like a little figure made of ice—you can clasp it in your hand and try to warm it up; then it will lose all its shape and sense, but the frozen sounds will melt a little and perhaps someone will hear them.

MARIA STEPANOVA

New Directions Paperbooks—a partial listing

Siegfried Lenz, The German Lesson
Alexander Lernet-Holenia, Count Luna
Denise Levertov, Selected Poems
Li Po, Selected Poems
Clarice Lispector, The Hour of the Star
  The Passion According to G. H.
Federico García Lorca, Selected Poems*
Nathaniel Mackey, Splay Anthem
Xavier de Maistre, Voyage Around My Room
Stéphane Mallarmé, Selected Poetry and Prose*
Javier Marías, Your Face Tomorrow (3 volumes)
Adam Mars-Jones, Box Hill
Bernadette Mayer, Midwinter Day
Carson McCullers, The Member of the Wedding
Fernando Melchor, Hurricane Season
Thomas Merton, New Seeds of Contemplation
  The Way of Chuang Tzu
Henri Michaux, A Barbarian in Asia
Dunya Mikhail, The Beekeeper
Henry Miller, The Colossus of Maroussi
  Big Sur & the Oranges of Hieronymus Bosch
Yukio Mishima, Confessions of a Mask
  Death in Midsummer
Eugenio Montale, Selected Poems*
Vladimir Nabokov, Laughter in the Dark
  Nikolai Gogol
Pablo Neruda, The Captain's Verses*
  Love Poems*
Charles Olson, Selected Writings
George Oppen, New Collected Poems
Wilfred Owen, Collected Poems
Hiroko Oyamada, The Hole
José Emilio Pacheco, Battles in the Desert
Michael Palmer, Little Elegies for Sister Satan
Nicanor Parra, Antipoems*
Boris Pasternak, Safe Conduct
Octavio Paz, Poems of Octavio Paz
Victor Pelevin, Omon Ra
Georges Perec, Ellis Island
Alejandra Pizarnik
  Extracting the Stone of Madness
Ezra Pound, The Cantos
  New Selected Poems and Translations
Raymond Queneau, Exercises in Style
Qian Zhongshu, Fortress Besieged
Herbert Read, The Green Child
Kenneth Rexroth, Selected Poems
Keith Ridgway, A Shock

Rainer Maria Rilke
  Poems from the Book of Hours
Arthur Rimbaud, Illuminations*
  A Season in Hell and The Drunken Boat*
Evelio Rosero, The Armies
Fran Ross, Oreo
Joseph Roth, The Emperor's Tomb
Raymond Roussel, Locus Solus
Ihara Saikaku, The Life of an Amorous Woman
Nathalie Sarraute, Tropisms
Jean-Paul Sartre, Nausea
Judith Schalansky, An Inventory of Losses
Delmore Schwartz
  In Dreams Begin Responsibilities
W. G. Sebald, The Emigrants
  The Rings of Saturn
Anne Serre, The Governesses
Patti Smith, Woolgathering
Stevie Smith, Best Poems
  Novel on Yellow Paper
Gary Snyder, Turtle Island
Dag Solstad, Professor Andersen's Night
Muriel Spark, The Driver's Seat
Maria Stepanova, In Memory of Memory
Wislawa Szymborska, How to Start Writing
Antonio Tabucchi, Pereira Maintains
Junichiro Tanizaki, The Maids
Yoko Tawada, The Emissary
  Memoirs of a Polar Bear
Dylan Thomas, A Child's Christmas in Wales
  Collected Poems
Tomas Tranströmer, The Great Enigma
Leonid Tsypkin, Summer in Baden-Baden
Tu Fu, Selected Poems
Paul Valéry, Selected Writings
Enrique Vila-Matas, Bartleby & Co.
Elio Vittorini, Conversations in Sicily
Rosmarie Waldrop, The Nick of Time
Robert Walser, The Assistant
  The Tanners
Eliot Weinberger, An Elemental Thing
  The Ghosts of Birds
Nathanael West, The Day of the Locust
  Miss Lonelyhearts
Tennessee Williams, The Glass Menagerie
  A Streetcar Named Desire
William Carlos Williams, Selected Poems
Louis Zukofsky, "A"

*BILINGUAL EDITION

For a complete listing, request a free catalog from New Directions, 80 8th Avenue, New York, NY 10011
or visit us online at **ndbooks.com**